RECOVERED
BODY

RECOVERED
BODY

Poems by Scott Cairns

GEORGE BRAZILLER PUBLISHER
New York

Eighth Day Press, 2838 East Douglas, Wichita, Kansas 67214
Originally published: George Braziller, Inc., © 1998.

Cover photo by Ze Farha
Cover design by NetWerx Creative, Inc.

SECOND EDITION

Library of Congress Cataloging-in-Publication Data:
Cairns, Scott.
RECOVERED BODY: POEMS / BY SCOTT CAIRNS
ISBN 0-9717483-4-9
LCCN 2003111683

Acknowledgments

Grateful acknowledgment is made to the following magazines where the poems listed below first appeared:

Ascent: "The Estuary"

Chariton Review: "The Death of Moses," "The Sacrifice of Isaac," and "At Grips with Jacob"

Columbia: "YHWH's Image"

Corona: "Alexandrian Fragments"

Image: A Journal of Arts and Religion: "The Entrance of Sin," "Solomon's Erotic Imagination," "Jonah's Imprisonment," "In the Well of Joseph's Brief Despair," "Into Hell and Out Again," and "To Himself"

Mars Hill Review: "In Lieu of Logos"

The Paris Review: "Necropolitan," "Loves," "The More Earnest Prayer of Christ," "Interval with Erato," "The Forest of the Stylites," and "Tesserae"

Prairie Schooner: "Musée," "Mr. Stevens Observes the Beach," "Archaeology: A Subsequent Lecture," "Regarding the Body," "Another Crucifixion," and "Exile"

Tailwind: "Short Trip to the Edge"

Weber Studies: "In the Minds of Three Sisters"

Western Humanities Review: "Deep Below Our Violences"

"Exile" and "The More Earnest Prayer of Christ" have also been anthologized in *Upholding Mystery*, Oxford University Press, 1996.

"To Himself" has also appeared in *Best Spiritual Writing 1998*, HarperCollins, 1998.

Bible quotations are from *The TANAKH: The New JPS Translation According to the Traditional Hebrew Text*. Copyright 1985 by the Jewish Publication Society. Used by permission.

Special thanks to Richard Howard and Janet Sylvester.

for my brother

Contents

III.

SUPPLICATIONS

Love Him in the World of the Flesh;
And at your marriage all its occasions shall dance for joy.
                    —W. H. Auden, from "For the Time Being"

NECROPOLITAN

Not your ordinary ice cream, though the glaze
of these skeletal figures affects
the disposition of those grinning candies
one finds in Mexico, say, at the start of November,
though here, each face is troublingly familiar,
exhibits the style adopted just as one declines
any further style—nectar one sips just as he
draws his last, dispassionate breath, becomes
citizen of a less earnest electorate. One learns
in that city finally how to enjoy a confection,
even if a genuine taste for this circumstance
has yet to be acquired, even if it is oneself
whose sugars and oils now avail a composure
which promises never to end, nor to alter.

I.

DEEP BELOW
OUR VIOLENCES

ALEXANDRIAN FRAGMENTS

after the fire

In those uncertain hours following our famous
conflagration, I surveyed with no small measure
of chagrin the scorched rubble, the thousand thousand

scroll rods charred and emptied of all but ashen curls,
steaming parchment, the air bitter and far too hot,
our book vaults fallen, the books reduced to cinder.

And in that moment the sun first lit our city's
eastern quarter, I found myself alone, in awe:
from that ruin, a forest had sprung up overnight,

as a wavering expanse of smoke white trees, pale
birches, original as the local laurel,
but shifting with the morning's faintest breath. They rose

to where their reaching branches twined to canopy
our broad destruction, so that each trunk expanded
at its uppermost and wove a fabric overhead—

now white, now red, now golden from the sun's approach.
Beneath that winding sheet our ravished corpus lay
razed, erased, an open, emptied volume in repose

insisting either new and strenuous reply,
or that we confess our hopelessness and turn away.

ARCHAEOLOGY: A SUBSEQUENT LECTURE

You're thinking that the present site favors
a broad expanse of fallow farmland more
than it does a fallen city. Let that be Lesson One.

The city is there, and none too deep. Soon
as we begin, you'll be surprised how thin
the veil turns out to be. You'll be surprised

how much survives interment, how little
survives intact. For the most part, our city
comes out in pieces, puzzling as any

deliberately jigsawed for an evening's
entertainment. And as you might have heard
(if not, here's Lesson Two) the pleasure lies

in fingering loose ends toward likely shape,
actually *making something* of these bits
of persons, places, things one finds once one

commences late interrogation
of undervalued, overlooked terrain—
what we in the business like to call *the dig*.

Musée

The old masters? Seldom wrong about *anything*,
never quite able to admit it when they were.

Notice, please, the execution of the wretched figure

That, I suppose, is the most fraught disadvantage
in *being* master, especially an old one.

all but veiled by chiaroscuro and the prominence

Still, when it came to suffering, they had the most
reliable perspective, compelling credentials.

of the winged tormentors whose features nearly radiate

They came to it, as they came to everything else—
practice, repetition, unwavering habit.

with pleasure taken in such consummate facility

O, long before they seemed anything like masters
they had come to observe every human torment

with the ivory hooks, and with the glinting, brazen,

as the fortunate occasion (they *were* masters)
for their most passionate renderings.

long-shaft pikes with which they daub the matter near the signature.

Deep Below Our Violences

Hard to describe, really—little light, no sense
of direction, and a persistent hum
which is almost Tibetan in its rhythms,

its repetition, its *human cum insect* tenor.
Still, there is a path, and though you must
take it with no indication of progress,

you come to believe that things look better
in transit. So you keep going, alert
to any clue as to how things *down here*

translate into the mess *up there*, any
possibility that some adjustment
at the hidden base of things might result

in better manners up top where it counts.

Back up in daylight, things are pretty much
how you left them. In a general, average way,
the permanence of the well-fed running

roughshod over the prostrate many
becomes a little hard to watch. The giddy
bloodlettings and pummelings one likes

to euphemize into *regional conflict*
have acquired a predictability
you'd just as soon be wrong about.

And you come to suspect that events so
common, universally available,
are incorrectly taken as local color.

Up or down, it's all pretty much a puzzle,
and such requests as *the heart of the matter*
or *the root cause* may be best left to those

who like their fictions pretending to be otherwise.

MR. STEVENS OBSERVES THE BEACH

Quite pleasant in its way, its deeply sad,
largely inarticulate way. And what
is that in the air? Some faint and fleeting

eau de decay? Low tide in our shallow bay.
Say, you've got a look about you that suggests
something nearly tropic on your mind.

Listen! A dozen *shes* singing at the shore!
But singing such cacophony you might
mistake the song for some mere calling home

of errant boys, or common hollering
in a game of volleyball, or just loud talk.
A fortunate boundary, don't you think?—

this ample stretch confusing sand and sea.
I like it best just after a good storm
when everything is changed—the wrack

and wreckage newly rearranged, the beach itself
retrenched along an unexpected line.
You can walk for hours before you meet the signs

insisting that the shore is property,
purchased (with a lien) and posted to attempt
some wish for privacy. They don't mean much.

Turn back if you will, I like walking there
best of all, where the illusion of ownership—
soon enough recensed by size 12 loafers—

gives way to more productive misperception.
The lighthouse at the point is miles farther
than it looks. Our sunlight is so keen

it pricks the simplest observation. Down
the windswept margin human figures,
dogs, beached boats, our tufted yellow grasses,

the very dunes, *all* waver in the heat,
all seem—so long as you squint in your approach—
to verge on something large indeed. The sea

has a numbing sort of genius, which it flaunts.
Not far inland, the earth's fixations strike
their grinning pose, frankly idiotic;

but here, where substances continue making
daily messes of all *things*, where even I
each day discover I am made to make

another set of fresh concessions which,
so long as no one's listening, I like to sing
with some measure of abandon into wind.

INTERVAL WITH ERATO

That's what I like best about you, Erato sighed in bed, *that's why
you've become one of my favorites and why you will always be so.*
I grazed her ear with my tongue, held the salty lobe between my lips.

I feel like singing when you do that, she said with more than a hint
of music already in her voice. *So sing,* I said, and moved down
to the tenderness at the edge of her jaw. *Hmmm,* she said, *that's nice.*

Is there anything you don't *like?* I asked, genuinely meaning
to please. *I don't like poets in a hurry,* she said, shifting
so my lips might achieve the more dangerous divot of her throat.

Ohhhh, she said, as I pressed a little harder there. She held my face
in both hands. *And I hate when they get careless, especially
when employing second-person address.* She sat up, and my mouth

fell to the tip of one breast. *Yes,* she said, *you know how it can be—
they're writing "you did this" and "you did that" and I always assume,
at first, that they mean* me! She slid one finger into my mouth to tease

the nipple there. *I mean it's disappointing enough to observe
the lyric is addressed to someone else, and* then, *the poet spends
half the poem spouting information that the* you—*if she or he

were listening—would have known already, ostensibly as well as,
or better than, the speaker.* I stopped to meet her eyes. *I know just
what you mean,* I said. She leaned down to take a turn, working my chest

with her mouth and hands, then sat back in open invitation.
Darling, she said as I returned to the underside of her breast,
have you noticed how many poets talk to themselves, about themselves?

I drew one finger down the middle of her back. *Maybe they fear*
no one else will hear or care. I sucked her belly, cupped her sopping
vulva with my hand. *My that's delicious,* she said, lifting into me.

Are all poets these days so lonely? She wove her fingers with mine
so we could caress her there together. *Not me,* I said, and ran
my slick hands back up to her breasts. I tongued her thighs. I said, *I'm not*

lonely now. She rubbed my neck, *No, dear, and you shouldn't be.*
  She clenched, *Oh!*
a little early bonus, she said; *I like surprises.* Then, *so*
few poets appreciate surprises, so many prefer to speak

only what they, clearly, already know, or think they know. If I
were a poet…well, I wouldn't be one at all if I hadn't
found a way to get a little something for myself—something new

from every outing, no? Me neither, I said, if somewhat indistinctly.
Oh! she said. *Yes!* she said, and tightened so I felt her pulse against
my lips. She lay quietly for a moment, obviously thinking.

Sweetie, she said, *that's what I like best about you—you pay attention,*
and you know how to listen when a girl feels like a little song.
Let's see if we can't find a little something now, especially for you.

THE SUBTLER EXILES

A little etymology can do a lot of harm.
    Turn over any cornerstone you'll find a thousand roots—
Any one of which might prove to be fun pulling up, if sure
    To cause a problem for the Post Office, hardly a treat
For the little tree. Still, exile has its advantages,
    Not the dullest of which is the lip-smacking circumstance
Of owing nothing to anything or anybody—
    A banal flavor of freedom, to be sure, but a taste
One might easily enough acquire through repetition.
    Being oppressed by snake worshipers is a real drag,
But asserting clear title to disputed wilderness
    Won't often result in quiet mornings over tea.
I'd hoped for indication of my getting somewhere,
    Which is probably about as likely as nostalgia.
There are other words for most of this. You can look them up.
    I found myself saying once how even a simple gesture
Winds up pointing fingers, shirking responsibility;
    But even *that* turns out a surprising disappointment
Once you've finished talking and the term is far from over.
    So, I've set off again, this time striking out as naked
As I can manage—which is to say, I remain pretty well
    Covered up, greatly burdened, oblivious to most of it.

THE ESTUARY

Turns out to have been the only way in,
at least the only way in from where
I began—a river pier extending

from borrowed shore beneath a rented house.
Here, the river's current meets the greater
pressures of the bay. As if unwilling

to accept its mingling dissolution,
the river seems to turn against itself,
to boil up into a rage, which makes

you stop and think before you dare to cross
this riptide in your little boat. *Me?* I kept
the outboard engine roaring in reverse,

not to retreat, exactly, mostly just
to hold my place until progress appeared
more possible. Out beyond the trouble

just before me, the blue expanse lay calm,
and farther out a dozen little boats
sat strangely fixed, their white sails slack, but you

weren't looking for allegory here, so
let's agree that the boats were real boats, that
they lay utterly still upon blue water,

and that for all this unsettling lack
something out there opened to the eye,
something rose and brooded still above the bay,

and in its mute immensity held that span
beyond the bar, where the larger body
met, absorbed our little estuary.

In the Minds of Three Sisters

1. The Believer

Her father has now *gone to be with God,* and so
this emptiness—the body—means very little,
left, as it is, so utterly behind, almost
beneath the dignity of her attention.
She looks from one weeping witness to the other,
and though she is also weeping, she asks them
with her eyes, *Why do you weep? He is not here.*

2. The Unbeliever

This stillness is unbearable, but she will bear it,
will find in time a manner of recalling
the man's dissolution as complete, something
of a relief. He is surely not *beyond* pain,
but the pain is gone—as the life is gone—and his
body rests, cooling, glazed with the last evidence,
last oils, of an impossibly wearied engine.

3. The Other

As he shuts down for good, the room itself goes slack.
What pain he knew has leapt into her throat, and so
she swallows it, and keeps it there to grow into
a kind of dread. She alone will set her lips to his,
and smooth his face, and will retain this bleak tableau
as first communion with the flesh, and with the dire
puzzlement the body held, holds, insinuates.

REGARDING THE BODY

I too was a decade coming to terms
with how abruptly my father had died.
And still I'm lying about it. His death
was surely as incremental, slow-paced
as any, and certainly as any
I'd witnessed. Still, as we met around him
that last morning—none of us unaware
of what the morning would bring—I was struck
by how quickly he left us. And the room
emptied—comes to me now—far too quickly.
If impiety toward the dead were still
deemed sin, it was that morning our common
trespass, to have imagined too readily
his absence, to have all but denied him
as he lay, simply, present before us.

A LIFE WITH ERATO

Dear, she said one day, *I'm weary of all the petty coherences*
the public life demands. By then, I'd grown used to paying
close attention whenever she spoke, and certainly whenever she spoke

in that melancholy tone. *Yes, love,* I said, and saw immediately
how right she was. *Nothing's so futile,* I agreed, *as those scores of*
    happenstance
hoping to pass themselves off as the big picture. It breaks your heart, really.

And it must be—I was thinking—far tougher for her, petitioned
as she was by endless requests from haggard men and women who,
for the most part, smoked and drank too much, by and large looked like
    shit,

or, at best, looked as though they'd look like shit very soon. Nearly all
had sour breath, grim dispositions, and a degree of neediness that turned
    out,
finally, to be insatiable. Never, it seemed, did it occur to a single one to
    just shut up.

I heard it all too, of course (I seldom left her side), but it must have
    been far
harder for her, always saying no, knowing they wouldn't hear even that,
but would press on with their doomed compositions until, because they
    were

so many, their exhausted discourse became the fashion, if a dowdy one
    at that,
and threatened to obliterate from view the more, say, spirited work our
    coupling
bore; and, well, it has made for more than a few disappointments over
    the years.

But I've got to tell you, coming home to a woman like that has a way of making light
any disillusion in the world at large. She sang. I heard my own voice rise to meet her.
Let's say that the veiled alcove of the private life offered ample compensation.

II.

THE RECOVERED MIDRASHIM
OF RABBI SAB

Regarding the sage whom tradition has come to identify as Rabbi Sab, very little is known, though a great deal is suspected. He was apparently a learnéd man whose devotion to *The One Whose Name Is Not Spoken* did not preclude his speaking that name frequently, and more often than not accompanied by a tone of accusation. He himself has been accused of apostasy, blasphemy, manic-depression, drunkenness, bad manners. He has been praised for his compassion, revered—if not much liked—for his eager upbraiding of the pious. While most forgive him his denunciations, few forgive him his glee. As to whether the emanation of the dual Torah extends to comprehend even these recovered commentaries, opinions vary.

YHWH's Image

And YHWH sat in the dust, bone weary after days of strenuous making, during which He, now and again, would pause to consider the way things were shaping up. Time also would pause upon these strange durations; it would lean back on its haunches, close its marble eyes, appear to doze.

And God said, "Let us make man in our image, after our likeness."
—Genesis 1.26

But when YHWH Himself finally sat on the dewy lawn—the first stage of his work all but finished—He took in a great breath laced with all lush odors of creation. It made him almost giddy.

As He exhaled, a sigh and sweet mist spread out from him, settling over the earth. In that obscurity, YHWH sat for an appalling interval, so extreme that even Time opened its eyes, and once, despite itself, let its tail twitch. Then YHWH lay back, running His hands over the damp grasses, and in deep contemplation reached into the soil, lifting great handsful of trembling clay to His lips, which parted to avail another breath.

With this clay He began to coat His shins, cover His thighs, His chest. He continued this layering, and, when He had been wholly interred, He parted the clay at His side, and retreated from it, leaving the image of Himself to wander in what remained of that early morning mist.

THE ENTRANCE OF SIN

Yes, there was a tree, and upon it, among the wax leaves, an order of fruit which hung plentifully, glazed with dew of a given morning. And there had been some talk off and on—nothing specific—about forgoing the inclination to eat of it. But sin had very little to do with this or with any outright prohibition.

The man said, "The woman You put at my side—she gave me of the tree, and I ate."
—Genesis 3.12

For sin had made its entrance long before the serpent spoke, long before the woman and the man had set their teeth to the pale, stringy flesh, which was, it turns out, also quite without flavor. Rather, sin had come in the midst of an evening stroll, when the woman had reached to take the man's hand and he withheld it.

In this way, the beginning of our trouble came to the garden almost without notice. And in later days, as the man and the woman wandered idly about their paradise, as they continued to enjoy the sensual pleasures of food and drink and spirited coupling, even as they sat marveling at the approach of evening and the more lush approach of sleep, they found within themselves a developing habit of resistance.

One supposes that, even then, this new taste for turning away might have been overcome, but that is assuming the two had found the result unpleasant. The beginning of loss was this: every time some manner of beauty was offered and declined, the subsequent isolation each conceived was irresistible.

THE TURNING OF LOT'S WIFE

First of all, she had a name, and she had a history. She was *Marah,* and long before the breath of death's angel turned her to bitter dust, she had slipped from her mother's womb with remarkable ease, had moved in due time from infancy to womanhood with a manner of grace that came to be the sole blessing of her aging parents. She was beloved.

And like most daughters who are beloved by both a mother and a father, Marah moved about her city with unflinching compassion, tending to the dispossessed as if they were her own. And they became her own. In a city given to all species of excess, there were a great many in agony—abandoned men, abandoned women, abandoned children. Upon these she poured out her substance and her care.

Her first taste of despair was at the directive of the messengers, who announced without apparent sentiment what was to come, and what was to be done. With surprising banality, they stood and spoke. One coughed dryly into his fist and would not meet her eyes. And one took a sip from the cup she offered before he handed it back and the two disappeared into the night.

Unlike her husband—coward and sycophant—the woman remained faithful unto death. For even as the man fled the horrors of a city's conflagration, outrunning Marah and

As the sun rose upon the earth and Lot entered Zoar, the Lord rained upon Sodom and Gomorrah sulfurous fire from the Lord out of heaven. He annihilated those cities and the entire Plain, and all the inhabitants of the cities and the vegetation of the ground. Lot's wife looked back, and she thereupon turned into a pillar of salt.
—Genesis 19.23–26

both girls as they all rushed into the desert, the woman stopped. She looked ahead briefly to the flat expanse, seeing her tall daughters, whose strong legs and churning arms were taking them safely to the hills; she saw, farther ahead, the old man whom she had served and comforted for twenty years. In the impossible interval where she stood, Marah saw that she could not turn her back on even one doomed child of the city, but must turn her back instead upon the saved.

THE SACRIFICE OF ISAAC

Who among us could bear the memory of Abraham's knife as it entered the heart of his son? Few enough, presumably. For why else has that incommensurate tableau been misrepeated so thoroughly?

In the stillness of that hour, the Lord pressed his servant inexplicably far and despite the gentled features of a great many fables thereafter—the angel's intercession, the convenient goat, *et cetera*—the knife did find its cramping sheath there in the boy's bared breast, and blood covered both the boy and the father who embraced him even then, and blood colored the rock altar, rouged the mire underfoot.

In pity, then, the Lord briefly withheld time's aberrant fall, retracted the merest portion of its descent, sparked a subsequent visitation of the scene. This time, he stayed the hand, the knife, the rush of blood and of horror, but only in time.

Just outside time's arch embarrassment—in the spinning swoon of the I Am—the boy is bloodied still upon the rock, the man fallen upon him, left with nothing but his extreme, his absolute, his dire obedience.

They arrived at the place of which God had told him. Abraham built an altar there; he laid out the wood; he bound his son Isaac; he laid him on the altar, on top of the wood. And Abraham picked up the knife to slay his son.
—*Genesis 22.9–10*

At Grips with Jacob

As the Angel of the Lord stooped to a little sport with the liar, He could not help but smile at how excessively the man struggled, as if he had a chance. And the Angel of the Lord was well pleased by how adroitly Jacob scuttled about in the dust, intent upon finding sufficient leverage, which, of course, he could not do.

During which time the Angel of the Lord continued to assume the man would eventually tire, finally give in to what was obvious, the impossibility of success.

So, when after many days Jacob's tenacity showed no promise of decline, when the Angel of the Lord began to stare a little glassy-eyed at yet another approach by his unlikely rival, when, after having tossed Jacob to his back for the upteenth time, the man took yet another tack, the Angel of the Lord put an end to the annoyance, hobbling Jacob with a single tap at the hip.

Jacob's sudden agony was a surprise to both. And as the man spun in the dust, tearing up great fistful of earth, the Angel of the Lord came to suspect a manner of suffering He had not known.

And thereafter, when He had set the hip right, when Jacob lay sleeping, his brow finally smoothed by ease and calming dreams, the Angel of the Lord continued

Jacob was left alone. And a man wrestled with him until the break of dawn. When he saw that he had not prevailed against him, he wrenched Jacob's hip at its socket, so that the socket of his hip was strained as he wrestled with him. Then he said, "Let me go, for dawn is breaking." But he answered, "I will not let you go, unless you bless me."
—Genesis 32.25–27

watching, admiring the phenomenon of change, keeping His own counsel as He speculated on the compensating aftermath of anguish, and the man's astonishing ability to be made whole.

In the Well of Joseph's Brief Despair

From that chill floor whose cloying mud became a numbing garment, the young man saw the world above poised as a pale blue pool—remote and indifferent—which, rather than reflecting any semblance of himself, seemed rather to absorb just about everything—all light, all hope, his future. He had tried climbing out, had tried calling for mercy, but each failure had left him more weary, disheartened, more thickly coated with mud.

And in that airless space the taunts and accusations from above also became increasingly confused, so that words became less, less like objects, more like unfortunate weather. Finally, exhausted and utterly without resort, Joseph slid back to the clay, giving in to the pressure of the blue pool held above him, falling silent as its trembling aspect became an abysmal amplitude.

Then he was lifted out, haggled over, and sold for a meager sum, during which time he could neither struggle nor speak. The journey into Egypt was one long study of the sky without conclusion.

And in succeeding years, through their provocative turns of fortune—false accusations, a little stretch in prison, a developing facility with dreams—Joseph came gradually into his own, famously forgave his own, pretty much had the last laugh, save when, always as late in the day as he could manage, he gave in to sleep

When Joseph came up to his brothers, they stripped Joseph of his tunic, the ornamented tunic that he was wearing, and took him and cast him into the pit. —Genesis 37.23–24

and to the return of that blue expanse, before
which all accretion—accomplishment, embell-
ishment, all likely interpretations—would drop
away as he found himself again in the hollow of
that well, naked, stunned, his every power spin-
ning as he lay, and looked, and swam.

THE DEATH OF MOSES

And in the interval of rest following the Father's tedious conversations with Moses, His own anger at the little man's blithe insubordination became nearly uncontrollable. And the Lord determined to kill the man, thereafter to undertake a more likely deliverance for His people.

Of course, Moses was instantly dead—his insistence upon remaining upright, walking about, chattering on with the innkeeper notwithstanding. For who can live, even briefly, beyond the forbearance of the Lord?

And if he lay dozing after a big meal of charred lamb and crushed mint, and if he lay dreaming of the innkeeper's well-fed wife, who would dare propose that any of these incidentals serve as evidence of life? That he was, despite appearances, breathless is articulated by his ability to sleep at all after such unpleasantness with the Father. He dreamed many dreams— vast chasms, pouring vortices, a single ram tethered to a post of limestone—none of them the dreams of the living.

As we are told, the Lord soon repented of His momentary whim, retracted the death, and, unbeknownst to the man—who, tradition has it, ordered a big breakfast and went his way as if nothing much had happened, pinching the innkeeper's wife on his way out the door— returned Moses to his place among the many other volatile shadows.

The Lord said to Moses in Midian, "Go back to Egypt, for all the men who sought to kill you are dead." So Moses took his wife and sons, mounted them on an ass, and went back to the land of Egypt; and Moses took the rod of God with him....

At a night encampment on the way, the Lord encountered Moses and sought to kill him.
—Exodus 4.19–20, and 24

Solomon's Erotic Imagination

To what purpose is the extravagant beauty of the body? To what purpose the lush accompaniment of two bodies drawn into a single contemplation? Solomon, our greatest poet and our king, could not for all his wisdom come to final understanding—for which we are grateful both to Solomon and to the Lord—but came instead to chance elaboration cast in song.

The woman (consider her form and consider what to Solomon would have seemed her implicit willingness) stood before him only once, and, because she was unaccustomed to such attention and because he was stunned into uncharacteristic humility, she stood before him only briefly before she retrieved her robe from where it lay at her feet, slipped back into it, and, promising to return when she was feeling a little braver, exited the tent.

Such modest exposure may not seem much, but for Solomon it proved plenty. And subsequently all of creation—the labor of bees, spice-scented evergreens, the heartrending, frolicking leap of twin deer—spun into serving a manner of expression whose sole outcome was to utter its own insufficiency. For though his song exceeds all songs in addressing the beauty of the woman, it falls silent at its conclusion, as it must, having offered only another manner of poverty *in lieu* of the woman, which it could not touch.

*Oh, give me the kisses of
   your mouth,
For your love is more
   delightful than wine.
Your name is like finest
   oil—
Therefore do maidens
   love you.
Draw me after you, let
   us run!
The king has brought me
   to his chambers.
Let us delight and rejoice
   in your love,
Savoring it more than
   wine—
Like new wine....*
   *—The Song of Songs
   1.2–4*

JEPHTHAH'S PIETY

One shouldn't be surprised at the wealth of explication our captain has provoked—wishful postulations about reprieve, anachronistic constructions of virgin orders, other hedgings— uncanny as it is that our hero and onetime deliverer could be so rash as to strike a no-win deal with the Almighty, unseemly that he would jeopardize his own for a little leverage in war. Even so, like the unfortunate lot of military men who are, in general, given to confusing their own blood lust with the will of God, Jephthah returned from battle with the Children of Ammon not quite satisfied.

Covered with gore and swaggering into the courtyard—which was more than a little cluttered with a career's worth of spoils—the soldier's attention was fixed upon his own open door, eager to see what he could kill next.

As the small figure rushed out—her arms thrown wide, her legs churning—the man was already considering where he might land the blow, or the series of blows, depending upon his pleasure. There was a flashing instant in which he stopped short, stood flat-footed, and puzzled about the tiny throb of recognition which pulsed once or twice behind his eyes. That's when he was pleased that he had made his vow—no more, then, to consider.

Children are always dying, being killed—both in scripture and in fact—though it is our fond habit and protection to euphemize such ges-

And Jephthah made the following vow to the Lord: "If you deliver the Children of Ammon into my hands, then whatever comes out of the door of my house to meet me on my safe return from the Ammonites shall be the Lord's and shall be offered by me as a burnt offering." Jephthah crossed over to the Children of Ammon and attacked them, and the Lord delivered them into his hands....When Jephthah arrived at his home in Mizpah, there was his daughter coming out to meet him, with timbrel and dance!

—Judges 11.30–32 and 34

tures as *the Children of Ammon* into purely
racial information. Just as the girl reached her
father, he ran her through with his sword. As a
kind of mercy, he took off her head with a neat
trick, moving only his wrist, then entered our
house to be adored.

JONAH'S IMPRISONMENT

What might one then expect when fleeing the Lord's imperative? Well, an obstacle of one or another sort—uneasiness of mind, missed connections, ungenerous companions, perhaps an enormous fish.

That Jonah was without joy at the prospect of Nineveh is well recorded. Less famous is his disinclination for *any* intercourse with unbelievers, whom he, out of habit, identified as the unwashed. From birth, he had been protected from most embarrassments: body odor, poorly cooked food, substandard grammar. And so the Lord, in His compassion, undertook to deliver Jonah from his own sin—not fastidiousness *as such*, only Jonah's insistence upon it.

His time in the fish's belly was like death. At the very least it *smelled* like death to Jonah. In retrospect, the experience, fully imagined, might still provoke a necessary sense of how the body, unadorned by ointments, oils, or silk is little more than meat, mere meat for fishes. And if, in that confusion of digesting debris, Jonah chose to distinguish himself from other meat, he would have to come up with other criteria, and pretty soon.

Consider any brute swimmer driving with all his energies *against* the tide; notice how ineffectual (and potentially comic) the effort appears from the chalk white cliffs above.

The word of the Lord came to Jonah son of Amittai: Go at once to Nineveh, that great city, and proclaim judgment upon it; for their wickedness has come before Me. Jonah, however, started out to flee to Tarshish from the Lord's service.
—Jonah 1.1–3

Gross facts aside, the monster was Jonah's deliverance, a more than sufficient transportation to a more likely perspective, from which Jonah was then fully willing to embrace anybody.

EXILE

Here *exactly*—a little elbow room. Here, in this margin of poor housing, harsh climate, and unreliable municipal services—something of a breathing space.

Have you *seen* the faces of the wanderers? Even in the midst of lamentation (especially then), they are radiant, wide-eyed and weeping, open-mouthed, keening at the tops of their lungs, and delirious with joy and purpose.

Even as the familiar supplications for delivery ascend alongside the fragrance of the censers, even as their voices rise to astonishing volume, and a number of garments—for emphasis—are torn beyond repair, even as the ritual of despair attains unbearable pathos, the blesséd appear to be taking some pleasure in the whole affair.

They have *their* etymologies too, after all—Holiness finding at its root a taste for separateness, fragmentation, periodic disruption in the status quo. Of course they are wandering *toward* something, but not in any great hurry.

Soon enough, they will come upon a day when the journey is fully behind them, when their colorful tents will be rolled up for good and left to rot in some outbuilding. Soon enough, the carts and litters will decay, the herds grow fat and unused to travel. Soon enough, the land will pull them in to stay.

And of their exile? Nothing will remain except

the memory—fading even so—of a journey
and a life with few oppressive properties, a
daily jaunt unparceled by boundaries or
taxes—in short, an expansive excursion
expressed for a season between the demands of
heathen kings and that last, conclusive
embrace.

III.

SUPPLICATIONS

THE FOREST OF THE STYLITES

—for Warren Farha

The way had become unbearably slow, progress
imperceptible. Even his hunger had become
less, little more than a poorly remembered myth

of never quite grasped significance. And the field
he now glimpsed far ahead appeared as a failed
forest whose cedars—bleached and branchless—clearly reached

past the edge of his sight. Occasional, erratic
movement at the tops of a few distant trees spun
his bearings some, induced brief vertigo, recalled

to him his hunger, if as a wave of nausea,
which abated, then poured back as he drew near and the trees
transformed to pillars, each topped by an enormous

weathered flightless bird enshrouded in a rag.

To Himself

When in scripture we first meet God,
apparently He is talking to Himself,
or to that portion in His midst
which He has only lately quit
to avail our occasion.

In prayer, therefore, we become
most like Him, speaking what no one
else, if not He, will attend.
A book I borrowed once taught me
how in the midst of attendant

prayer comes a pause when The Addressed
requires nothing else be said. Yes,
I witnessed once an emptying
like that; though what I saw was not
quite seen, of course. I suspected

nonetheless a silent Other
silently regarding me as if He
still might speak, but speak as to Himself.
That was yesterday, or many
years ago, and if it profit

anyone to imitate the terms
of that exchange, let the prior
gesture be extreme hollowing
of the throat, an inclination
to articulate the trouble

of a word, a world thereafter.

THANKSGIVING FOR A HABIT

Thus unencumbered by method,
the dilettante exegete finds
ample occasion for discourse,

a habit of trusting the mind's
less architectural leanings,
especially troubling Time's

quaint and illusory pattern,
its pretense of ordering. I'm
guessing his happiest moments

occur in appalling, half blind,
otherwise mute speculation
when, glimpsing some textual bind,

he loosens his grip on the matter,
if briefly, recovers in time,
sees as he circumvents terror

a glimpse of enormity. My
best speculation proposes
that this is as close to sublime

matters as any would wish for
so long as one's still doing Time.

THE MORE EARNEST PRAYER OF CHRIST

And being in an agony he prayed more earnestly....
                    —Luke 22.44

His last prayer in the garden began, as most
of his prayers began—*in earnest*, certainly,
but not without distraction, an habitual...what?

Distance? Well, yes, a sort of distance, or a mute
remove from the genuine distress he witnessed
in the endlessly grasping hands of multitudes

and, often enough, in his own embarrassing
circle of intimates. Even now, he could see
these where they slept, sprawled upon their robes or wrapped

among the arching olive trees. Still, something new,
unlikely, uncanny was commencing as he spoke.
As the divine in him contracted to an ache,

a throbbing in the throat, his vision blurred, his voice
grew thick and unfamiliar; his prayer—just before
it fell to silence—became uniquely earnest.

And in that moment—perhaps because it was so
new—he *saw* something, had his first taste of what
he would become, first pure taste of the body, and the blood.

ANOTHER CRUCIFIXION

The last of the three to die was the one
whose harsh words to the rabbi had availed
for the third culprit the astonishing
promise of paradise.

The last of the three could no longer turn
even his head—his body had stiffened.
He did not dare close his eyes again, so
fixed upon the rabbi's face,

which had grown so utterly still, opaque,
that the dying one observed a vivid
mirroring of his own condition there,
or so he imagined,

confused, struggling to see anything clearly.
As that face blurred, he saw beyond to the one
whose shins were that moment cracking across
the flat of a sword.

That man, too, was clearly dead, and if this day
he also swam in bliss, it didn't show.
The dying man would examine the dead
rabbi one more time

if he could, but finally knew the man
was lost to his sight. He felt a tug, far
away (at his feet?) and a blade across
his knees. He heard them crack,

and heard himself cry out (so far away).
Dying, he thought that if he could just glimpse
the rabbi's ruined face, he might suspect
a kingdom even now.

LOVES

Magdalen's Epistle

Of Love's discrete occasions, we
observe sufficient catalogue,
a likely-sounding lexicon

pronounced so as to implicate
a wealth of difference, where reclines
instead a common element,

itself quite like those elements
partaken at the table served
by Jesus on the night he was

betrayed—like those in that the bread
was breakable, the wine was red
and wet, and met the tongue with bright,

intoxicating sweetness, quite
like…wine. None of what I write arrives
to compromise that sacrament,

the mystery of spirit graved
in what is commonplace and plain—
the broken, brittle crust, the cup.

Quite otherwise, I choose instead
to bear again the news that each,
each was still *itself*, substantial

in the simplest sense. By now, you
will have learned of Magdalen, a name
recalled for having won a touch

of favor from the one we call
the son of man, and what you've heard
is true enough. I met him first

as, mute, he scribbled in the dust
to shame some village hypocrites
toward leaving me unbloodied,

if ill-disposed to taking up
again a prior circumstance.
I met him in the house of one

who was a Pharisee and not
prepared to suffer quietly
my handling of the master's feet.

Much later, in the garden when,
having died and risen, he spoke
as to a maid and asked me why

I wept. When, at *any* meeting
with the Christ, was I not weeping?
For what? I only speculate

—brief inability to speak,
a weak and giddy troubling near
the throat, a wash of gratitude.

And early on, I think, some slight
abiding sense of shame, a sop
I have inferred more recently

to do without. Lush poverty!
I think that *this* is what I'm called
to say, this mild exhortation

that one should still abide *all* love's
embarrassments, and so resist
the new temptation—dangerous,

inexpedient mask—of shame.
And, well, perhaps one other thing:
I have received some little bit

about the glib divisions which
so lately have occurred to you
as right, as necessary, fit—

That the body is something less
than honorable, say, in its
...appetites? That the spirit is

something pure, and—if all goes well—
potentially unencumbered
by the body's bawdy tastes.

This disposition, then, has led
to a banal and pious lack
of charity, and, worse, has led

more than a few to attempt some
soul-preserving severance—harsh
mortifications, manglings, all

manner of ritual excision
lately undertaken to prevent
the body's claim upon the *heart*,

or *mind*, or (blasphemy!) *spirit*—
whatever name you fix upon
the supposéd *bodiless*.

I fear that you presume—dissecting
the person unto something less
complex. I think that you forget

you are not Greek. I think that you
forget the very issue which
induced the Christ to take on flesh.

All loves are bodily, require
that the lips part, and press their trace
of secrecy upon the one

beloved—the one, or many, endless
array whose aspects turn to face
the one who calls, the one whose choice

it was one day to lift my own
bruised body from the dust, where, it seems
to me, I must have met my death,

thereafter, this subsequent life
and late disinclination toward
simple reductions in the name

of Jesus, whose image I work
daily to retain. I have kissed
his feet. I have looked long

into the trouble of his face,
and met, in that intersection,
the sacred place—where body

and spirit both abide, both yield,
in mutual obsession. Yes,
if you'll recall your Hebrew *word*.

just long enough to glimpse in its
dense figure *power to produce*
you'll see as well the damage Greek

has wrought upon your tongue, stolen
from your sense of what is holy,
wholly good, fully animal—

the body which he now prepares.

TESSERAE

—for Marcia Vanderlip

In paling sixth-hour light the woman cups
one azure tile fragment as if asking
of its brokenness a sign. The bright

mosaic framed before her far
from finished, she tries positioning
the speck in mind before her hand inclines

to set the fraction as a sum. In time,
this mote of clay-returned-to-element
will serve as iris for the eye

of an impossibly tinted bird
whose gaudy elegance lies entirely
comprised of likewise shattered earthenware,

which, lifted from the heap, articulates
a second purpose, free from more mundane
practicalities, clearly out of nature

sprung into a flight of some duration.

In Lieu of Logos

Let's suppose some figure more Hebraic
in its promise, more inclined to move

from one provisional encampment
to the next, then discover the effect

wandering tenders even as it draws
the weary hiker on to further

speculation, crossing what has seemed so
like barren country but whose very

barrenness proves a prod for yet another
likely story. The old Jews liked *davar*,

which did something more than just point fingers
to what lies back behind one's fussy, Greek

ontology of diminishing
returns. I have come to like it too, *word*

with a future as dense as its past,
a *Ding Gedicht* whose chubby letters each

afford a pause at which the traveler
rubs his chin and looking up entertains

a series of alternate routes, just now
staying put at the borrowed outpost,

but marveling how each turn of the head
gives way to distance, layers every term

of travel—each terminal—with reprieve,
invites indeterminate, obscure enormity

to gather at the glib horizon's edge.

INTO HELL AND OUT AGAIN

In this Byzantine-inflected icon
of the Resurrection, the murdered Christ
is still in Hell, the chief issue being

that *this* Resurrection is of our agéd
parents and all their poor relations. We
find Him as we might expect, radiant

in spotless white, standing straight, but leaning
back against the weight of lifting them. Long
tradition has Him standing upon two

crossed boards—the very gates of Hell—and He,
by standing thus, has *undone Death by Death*,
we say, and saying nearly apprehend.

This *all*—the lifting of the dead, the death
of Death, His stretching here between two realms—
looks like real work, necessary, not pleasant

but almost matter-of-factly undertaken.
We witness here a little sheepishness
which death has taught both Mom and Dad; they reach

Christ's proffered hands and everything about
their affect speaks centuries of drowning
in that abysmal crypt. Are they quite awake?

Odd—motionless as they must be in our
tableau outside of Time, we almost see
their hurry. And isn't that their shame

which falls away? They have yet to enter bliss,
but they rise up, eager and a little shocked
to find their bodies capable of this.

Short Trip to the Edge

And then I was standing at the edge. It would surprise you
how near to home. And the abyss? Every shade of blue,
all of them readily confused, and, oddly, none of this
as terrifying as I had expected, just endless.

What? You find this business easy? When every breath is thick
with heady vapor from the edge? You might not be so quick
to deny what prefers its more dramatic churning done
out of sight. Enough about you. The enormity spun,

and I spun too, and reached across what must have been its dome.
When I was good and dizzy (since it was so near), I went home.